LAUGH-OUT-LOUD JOKES

LAUGH-OUT-LOUD SCHOOL JOKES

CAITIE MCANENEY

WINDMILL BOOKS

Published in 2025 by Windmill Books, an Imprint of Rosen Publishing
2544 Clinton St., Buffalo, NY 14224

First Edition

Editor: Caitie McAneney
Book Design: Claire Zimmermann

Photo Credits: Cover, p.1 (child laughing) Prostock-studio/Shutterstock.com; cover, pp. 1 (ruler, protractor, pencil, scissors, binder clips, and paint tube illustrations), 4, 6, 8, 10, 14, 18, 22, 23 (apple) JuulDu/Shutterstock.com; cover, pp. 1 (stack of books, colored pencils, and globe illustrations), 12, 16, 20, 23 (books) Nadzin/Shutterstock.com; series art (paper texture) OanaGherghe2/Shutterstock.com; p. 5 Aleksei Potov/Shutterstock.com; p. 7 Krakenimages.com/Shutterstock.com; p. 9 (main) Kuznetsov Alexey/Shutterstock.com; p. 9 (inset) slavantonov/Shutterstock.com; p. 11 KlingSup/Shutterstock.com; p. 13 Raul Mellado Ortiz/Shutterstock.com; p. 15 PeopleImages.com - Yuri A/Shutterstock.com; p. 17 Roman Samborskyi/Shutterstock.com; p. 19 Natali Kuzina/Shutterstock.com; p. 21 (main) jstudio/Shutterstock.com; p. 21 (inset) New Africa/Shutterstock.com.

Some of the images in this book illustrate individuals who are models. The depictions do not imply actual situations or events.

Library of Congress Cataloging-in-Publication Data

Names: McAneney, Caitie, author.
Title: Laugh-out-loud school jokes / Caitie McAneney.
Description: Buffalo : Windmill Books, 2025. | Series: Laugh-out-loud jokes | Includes index.
Identifiers: LCCN 2024010584 (print) | LCCN 2024010585 (ebook) | ISBN 9781538396865 (library binding) | ISBN 9781538396858 (paperback) | ISBN 9781538396872 (ebook)
Subjects: LCSH: School–Juvenile humor. | Wit and humor, Juvenile.
Classification: LCC PN6231.S3 M385 2025 (print) | LCC PN6231.S3 (ebook) | DDC 818/.602–dc23/eng/20240313
LC record available at https://lccn.loc.gov/2024010584
LC ebook record available at https://lccn.loc.gov/2024010585

Manufactured in the United States of America

CPSIA Compliance Information: Batch #CSWM25. For further information, contact Rosen Publishing at 1-800-237-9932

CONTENTS

Make the Grade! 4
Teacher Talk 6
Math Matters 8
Super Social Studies 10
Silly Science 12
Reading 14
Library Laughs 16
Gym Time 18
Music Notes 20
Glossary 22
For More Information 23
Index 24

Words in the glossary appear in **bold** the first time they are used in the text.

MAKE THE GRADE!

How do you get straight A's?

USE A RULER!

Where do pencils vacation each summer?

PENCIL-VANIA.

What did the paper say to the pen?

"WRITE ON!"

Why are calculators good friends to have?

YOU CAN ALWAYS COUNT ON THEM.

FUN FACT!

Pencil leads have no lead in them! The "lead" is actually **graphite** mixed with clay.

TEACHER TALK

What do teachers do at the beach?

TEST THE WATERS.

Why do teachers need sunglasses?

THEIR STUDENTS ARE SO BRIGHT!

Why did the teacher cross her eyes?

SHE COULDN'T CONTROL HER PUPILS.

What did the ghost teacher say to her students?

"OK, CLASS, LOOK AT THE BOARD. I'LL GO THROUGH IT AGAIN."

FUN FACT!

There are more than 1.5 million kindergarten and elementary school teachers in the United States. It's a popular job!

MATH MATTERS

What did the triangle say to the circle?

"YOU'RE POINTLESS."

Why was the math homework sad?

IT HAD A LOT OF PROBLEMS.

What did the number 0 say to 8?

"I LIKE YOUR BELT!"

How do you make seven even?

SUBTRACT THE S.

FUN FACT!

The "Father of Mathematics" is Archimedes, a mathematician from **ancient** Greece.

Archimedes

SUPER SOCIAL STUDIES

Did you hear the joke about the Liberty Bell?

YEP, IT CRACKED ME UP TOO!

What has 5 eyes and is full of water?

THE MISSISSIPPI RIVER.

How is history like a fruit cake?

IT'S FULL OF DATES.

Why did the globe get detention?

HE HAD A BAD LATITUDE.

FUN FACT!

The Mississippi River is one of the largest rivers in the world! It's the second longest in North America.

SILLY SCIENCE

Why did the cell cross the microscope?

TO GET TO THE OTHER SLIDE.

What's a computer's favorite snack food?

CHIPS.

Why are chemists good at dealing with problems?

THEY HAVE ALL THE SOLUTIONS.

How do you freshen your breath in science class?

EXPERI-MINTS!

FUN FACT!

The strongest microscope in the world can see individual **atoms**!

READING

Why did the elephant put his trunk in a book?

SO HE **NOSE** WHERE HE STOPPED READING!

What does a book wear when it gets cold?

A JACKET.

Why did the book go to the **chiropractor**?

IT HAD A PROBLEM WITH ITS SPINE.

What do you call a book about baby rabbits?

A HARE-RAISING TALE!

FUN FACT!

Dust jackets were invented to protect hardcover books from wear and tear. In **medieval** times, people wrapped books in silk, leather, or velvet.

LIBRARY LAUGHS

What do librarians bring on fishing trips?

BOOK WORMS.

What vegetables do librarians eat?

"QUIET PEAS!"

Where do librarians sleep?

BETWEEN THE COVERS!

What building has the most stories?

THE LIBRARY!

FUN FACT!

The Library of Congress in Washington, D.C., is the largest library on Earth.

GYM
TIME

Why was Cinderella picked last in soccer?

SHE ALWAYS RUNS AWAY FROM THE BALL.

Why did the turkey get benched during his basketball game?

TOO MUCH FOWL PLAY.

Do basketball players like cookies?

ONLY IF THEY CAN DUNK THEM!

What position do ghosts play in soccer?

GHOUL KEEPER.

FUN FACT!

Basketball is the most popular youth sport in the United States.

MUSIC NOTES

Why did the music teacher carry a ladder?

TO REACH THE HIGH NOTES.

How do you make a bandstand?

TAKE AWAY THE CHAIRS!

What's a difference between a piano and a fish?

YOU CAN TUNE A PIANO, BUT YOU CAN'T TUNA FISH!

What do you call a musician who breaks the rules?

A TREBLEMAKER.

FUN FACT!

Higher notes are written with the treble clef at the beginning of a line of music. Lower notes are written with a bass clef.

treble clef

GLOSSARY

ancient: From a long time ago.

atom: The smallest possible unit of a chemical element.

chiropractor: A person who treats disorders of the musculoskeletal system.

fowl: A bird that is raised for its eggs or meat.

graphite: A soft, black or gray form of carbon.

latitude: The distance between the equator and a point north or south on Earth's surface.

medieval: Having to do with the Middle Ages, a time in European history from about 500 CE to 1500 CE.

microscope: A tool used to view very small objects so they can be seen much larger and more clearly.

pupil: A student. Also, a small, dark opening in the center of the eye.

solution: The answer to a problem. Also, a chemical mixture of two or more substances.

FOR MORE INFORMATION

BOOKS

Franco, Michou. *I'm Going to Be a Teacher!* Buffalo, NY: Gareth Stevens Publishing, 2025.

McDonald, Amy. *School.* Minneapolis, MN: Bellwether Media Inc., 2022.

Sautter, Aaron. *Zany School Riddles.* North Mankato, MN: Pebble Books, 2024.

WEBSITES

Science
www.brainpop.com/science/
Learn fun facts about different science topics with BrainPop.

Social Studies Games
pbskids.org/games/social-studies
Make social studies super fun with these games from PBS Kids.

INDEX

Archimedes, 9

basketball, 18, 19

books, 14, 15, 16

calculators, 4

history, 10

Liberty Bell, 10

librarians, 16

Library of Congress, 17

math, 8, 9

medieval times, 15

microscopes, 12, 13

Mississippi River, 10, 11

music, 20, 21

science, 12

summer, 4

teachers, 6, 7, 20